What Was It Like Growing Up in the 80s?

A Journal to Revisit and Share the Totally Awesome 80s

~ Riya Aarini ~

What Was It Like Growing Up in the 80s?
A Journal to Revisit and Share the Totally Awesome 80s
Text Copyright © 2025 by Riya Aarini

ISBN: 978-1-956496-59-8 (paperback)
ISBN: 978-1-956496-60-4 (hardcover)

This book belongs to '80s kid

Contents

Welcome to Your '80s History!

The 1980s was a dreamy decade of excess. Materialism pervaded every inch of colorful societal fabric. Everything seemed fresh and intriguing—yet a sense of welcome honesty proliferated. Optimism ran high despite the threats of the Cold War hovering over everyone young and old. Youth grew up carefree, dressing and speaking as no other generation dressed and spoke before.

The era remains distinct, instantly recognizable, and unforgettable. It's no surprise that this generation feels a sense of nostalgia for the decade of their childhood and all things now termed "vintage."

Individuals who are products of the '80s flamboyant materialism can return to their cherished bygone years. Travel back in time by responding to the prompts in this journal—a literal time capsule to share with friends, significant others, and children who yearn to know what makes this decade so special.

Filling out this journal might stir up settled dust and reveal shiny parts that have long been buried. But by reflecting and sharing your unique and collective experiences with loved ones, the unsurpassed glories of the '80s live on. Here's to the riveting and dynamic '80s culture!

Birthdays

List five stellar birthday gifts you received in the '80s.

_____

_____

_____

_____

_____

Where did you celebrate your birthdays? Common '80s party venues included the roller rink, pizza parlor, park, at home.

How did you celebrate your birthdays in the '80s?

Did you host birthday slumber parties? If so, describe a totally tubular one.

Did you enjoy homemade birthday cakes or cakes from the bakery? If homemade, who baked them?

What did your party goodie bags include?

How did your party guests RSVP?

School

What was your favorite class?

Did you learn to type on a typewriter?

Did you use your school's computer lab? What did you use it for?

Did you pass handwritten notes in class?

Describe one of the funniest or most embarrassing.

Describe a time the teacher intercepted and read the note out loud.

How well did you perfect the origami-like folding?

What foods did school lunches consist of?

How much did a small carton of milk or chocolate milk cost?

Were you ever sent to detention? If so, why?

Extracurricular
Activities

What extracurricular activities did you participate in?

If you were in the school band, what instrument did you play?

If you were athletic, what sports did you play?

If you served on the school newspaper, what was your role?

Cursive

If you learned cursive in school, do you now feel privileged to be a part of one of the last generations to read and write cursive?

Libraries

How did you conduct library research for school projects?

What was your experience like thumbing through the library's tightly packed card catalog to find a book?

How intimidated did you feel by the 30-volume encyclopedia sets on the shelves?

Yearbooks

Did you sign your classmates' elementary, junior high, or high school yearbooks?

Do you recall any memorable messages, inside jokes, or well-wishes?

How important was it to you to autograph yearbooks or have yours autographed?

Graduation

How did it feel to graduate elementary school, middle school, or high school in the '80s?

Describe your graduation ceremony, if your school had one.

What are your best memories of graduation?

Friends

Did you have a few or many friends growing up in the '80s?

How did you bond with friends in the '80s? Movies, music, hobbies?

Did you host or attend sleepovers? What were they like?

Did you talk on a corded phone with friends?

If your home had one phone line, how limited in time were conversations?

Did you feel upset when the cord didn't stretch far?

How often did you go to the movies or drive-ins?

Did you negotiate with friends on which movies to rent, then watch them at their houses?

Was camp a part of your childhood? Describe the best and worst of camp.

How would you describe the quality of friendships in the '80s?

Friendship Bracelets

Did you weave friendship bracelets with colorful thread?

Did you exchange friendship bracelets? If so, with whom?

How many friendship bracelets did you wear at a time on your wrists?

What significance did friendship bracelets hold during your '80s childhood?

Fashion

What '80s fashion trend did you try and like?

What '80s fashion trend did you try and dislike?

Tie-dye Clothing

Tie-dye apparel, vibrantly hued, was a symbol of freedom and creativity.

Did you wear tie-dye T-shirts, shorts, or jackets in a spirit of youthful rebellion?

Did you make your own tie-dye clothing?

Shoulder Pads

Shoulder pads equalized the show of power between women and men.

Did your shirts and jackets come sewn with shoulder pads? How powerful did you feel wearing them?

As the shoulder-pad trend faded, what did you do with your clothing stitched with shoulder pads?

Leg Warmers

Did you wear leg warmers outside of aerobics or dance class?

If so, where did you pull off the trendy leg-warmers look?

What inspired you to don leg warmers?

Did you feel "cool" wearing leg warmers?

Hair

Hairspray

Hairspray might've single-handedly defined voluminous '80s hairstyles.

Did you apply generous amounts of hairspray to set gravity defying bangs?

Did you spray profusely to achieve the desirable feathered or mullet look?

Scrunchies

Did you tie up your big '80s hair in scrunchies?

Are you still enthusiastic about scrunchies, and do you wear them today?

Perms

Perms offered desirable volume to otherwise limp women's and men's hair.

Did you get dramatic perms in the '80s?

In the '80s, bigger was better. How bodacious did your perms get?

Mullets

What were your thoughts about the '80s mullet, known as business up front and a party in the back?

Did you wear a mullet? What influenced your decision?

Holidays

Valentine's Day

How did you celebrate the day of love in the '80s?

Did you pass out cardstock Valentine's Day cards to classmates?

Did you receive Valentine's Day cards from classmates? If so, do you still have them, such as in a box in the attic?

Did you decorate a Valentine's Day box to collect cards and candy?

July the Fourth

How did you celebrate Independence Day in the '80s?

Did you light sparklers or go big with fireworks?

Did you join or watch the Fourth of July parades? What sentiments did they inspire?

Halloween

List three gnarly Halloween costumes you wore in the '80s.

_____

_____

_____

Did you wear plastic or homemade costumes? If homemade, who sewed them?

Did you trick-or-treat? What did you use to collect candy: jack-o-lantern bucket, paper bag, pillow case?

What did you think about homes that gave out king-size candy bars?

What was your favorite Halloween candy? What was your least favorite?

Did you trade candy with fellow trick-or-treaters?

How did you feel when you received fast-food coupons in your trick-or-treat bag?

Did your parents impose a tax on your Halloween candy?

List one unusual thing you received while trick-or-treating.

How late did you stay out freely roaming the streets on Halloween night?

Did you play Ouija boards and Bloody Mary?

Did you watch Halloween specials on TV? If so, which ones?

What Halloween pranks did you plot on unsuspecting adults? Describe one!

How magical was Halloween in the '80s?

Politics

US Presidents

In 1980, how did you feel about the beginning of the Reagan era? What was it like having a former movie star as president?

What did you think about President Reagan appointing the first woman, Sandra Day O'Connor, to the Supreme Court in 1981?

Iran-Iraq War

Did you write current events reports in school about the Iran-Iraq War?

Tiananmen Square

What was your reaction to the turmoil surrounding Beijing's democratic protests in 1989?

Cold War

How did the Cold War shape your childhood, if at all?

Did the looming threat of the adversary pressing the "big red button" (nuclear annihilation) give you sleepless nights?

How moved were you by '80s songs about nuclear war?

Songs included
1983: "It's a Mistake" by Men at Work
1988: "Blackened" by Metallica
1989: "Leningrad" by Billy Joel

What did you think of the 1984 movie "Red Dawn," about teens fighting Soviet forces invading their Colorado town?

Was your school a fallout shelter?

Did you perform nuclear bomb drills in school?

What were your thoughts about the friendship between Soviet President Mikhail Gorbachev and US President Ronald Reagan?

Berlin Wall

How did you feel when the Berlin Wall fell in 1989, reuniting East and West Germany?

News

The internet and social media hadn't yet become commonplace, so people learned about local and world events through a variety of media.

Newspapers

Did your family buy newspapers from the newsstand or subscribe to home deliveries?

What did you think about the bundled, weighty newspapers and flipping through the fragile, grayish newsprint with coupons tucked inside?

Magazines

List three '80s magazines you bought individually or subscribed to.

_____

_____

_____

School

What '80s world events learned in class made the most impact on you?

Space Exploration

Did trailblazer, Sally Ride, the first American woman to launch into space, inspire you with her June 1983 mission aboard the Space Shuttle Challenger?

Were your eyes glued to the TV when NASA launched Space Shuttles Columbia in 1981, Challenger in 1983, and Discovery in 1984?

Did you skip school to watch the historic liftoffs, aired live, or did you watch them in class when the teacher wheeled in a TV?

How did you feel upon seeing the liftoffs? Awed, inspired, excited for the possibilities of space exploration?

What emotions ran through you when you saw or heard about the Challenger explosion?

Conversations

Did you enjoy the face-to-face conversations of the '80s?

Did you feel more connected to people (the music store clerk, strangers on the bus, or even friends) in the '80s?

Do you feel a sense of honesty permeated '80s conversations? If so, how?

Did you pepper your speech with popular '80s slang?

Do you catch yourself still using these words today?

Books

What were your top five books in the '80s?

_____

_____

_____

_____

_____

List your favorite book series.

Who were your favorite authors?

Did you perform extra chores to earn money to buy books?

How often did you visit the library to check out books?

Did you read a set number of books to earn coupons for a free personal pizza? If so, how did it feel to redeem the vouchers?

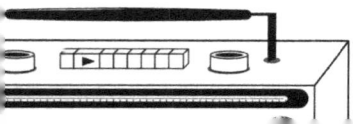

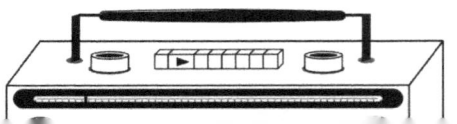

Music

Hairbands, glam rock, and flamboyant pop music dominated the '80s music scenes. Other musical genres that grew in popularity during the decade included new wave, adult contemporary, jazz, and electronic dance.

What were your favorite '80s music genres?

What musicians or bands did you enjoy most in the '80s?

List three songs you couldn't resist playing on repeat.

_____

_____

_____

If you listened to the radio, how did it feel when your favorite song played by chance?

Did you watch MTV or VH1?

What was it like watching bands perform in music videos?

Did you carry a boom box (and 20 batteries to power it up)?

Where did you listen to a Walkman, if you owned one?

Mixtapes

Did you create your own mixtapes?

How careful were you to hit pause to avoid recording commercials?

Did you give homemade mixtapes to friends?

Did you customize mixtapes with love songs and give them to crushes? If so, how did they respond?

Considering the time and effort it took to create mixtapes, what significance did they hold for you?

Staying Connected

Answering Machines

Did your family use an answering machine?

What was one of the funniest answering machine messages you'd heard?

Describe an answering machine fiasco.

Landlines

Did you dial friends and family using a push-button or a rotary phone?

Did you memorize friends' phone numbers?

Cell Phones

'80s cell phones weighed more than 10 pounds and cost almost $4K!

Did your family own a bulky, brick '80s cell phone?

If so, where did they carry it?

Pay Phones

Did you carry around quarters in case you needed to use a pay phone?

Did you wipe the greasy handset against your clothes to clean it before using?

Did you ever find coins in the coin return? How thrilled did you feel?

Did you ever call collect? Give an example of a time you asked the operator to make a collect call.

Did you receive calls at a payphone? If so, how did you arrange it, and who called you?

Phone Books

How often did you use the phone book? Whose numbers did you look up?

Did your family pay the phone book company to keep your number unlisted?

Did you comb through the phone book, looking for people with the same name as you?

Did you ever prank call someone using a number listed in the phone book? Describe the prank!

Letters

Did you write letters with pen or pencil on decorative stationery?

Describe a favorite letter you received.

Do you still have this letter, like in a keepsake box?

Greeting Cards

Describe one of the most memorable greeting cards you received in the '80s.

Did you give handmade greeting cards? If so, describe one.

Flashes from the '80s Past

Flashes from the '80s Past

Prom

Did you go to prom? If so, what did you wear? What did your date wear?

Did you go all out on prom night with a limo and fancy dinner? If not, what fun prom activities did you enjoy?

What lasting memories did prom celebrations create?

Did you take the traditional prom photo? Would you describe it as cringeworthy or memorable? What made it so?

What was your prom song?

Was it performed by a live band?

Dating

Where did you take your date? Or where did your date take you?

Did your date ask your parents for permission before taking you out?

Were you ever late to a date and missed the event (because you didn't yet have the convenience of texting that you were running behind)?

Did you receive mixtapes with romantic songs? What did they tell you about the giver?

Do you feel dating was simpler in the '80s? Why or why not?

Given the face-to-face interactions, do you believe dating was more authentic in the '80s?

Computers

Did your family own one of the first home computers?

If so, what type of computer was it?

How much did the computer cost?

What did you use the computer for?

Video Games

Did you play video games in the '80s? If so, on a home gaming console or at the arcades?

List your favorite video games.

How much time and how many quarters did you spend at the arcades?

Describe the '80s arcade experience.

Cameras

Did you use film cameras in the '80s?

Where did you develop the film?

How long did you wait for your roll of film to be developed?

How did it feel to finally receive the photos?

How excited were you about Polaroid cameras that produced instant printed photos?

Food

Everything was bigger in the '80s, including food portion sizes.

Did your family dine at all-you-can-eat buffets? For some families, this was a highly anticipated ritual.

What was your favorite buffet restaurant?

List the most appetizing buffet dishes.

As a kid, did you eat free at the buffets? How cool was that?

What was your favorite homecooked meal?

What were your favorite '80s snacks?

Celebrities

Who were your favorite celebrities in music, movies, or sports?

What did you admire about them?

Did you get to meet any of your favorite celebrities? If so, where?

Movies

Popular '80s movies included

1982: "ET"
1984: "Ghostbusters"
1985: "The Goonies"

List three epic '80s movies.

_____

_____

_____

Did you go to the local theater to watch movies?

Did you rent VHS tapes to watch movies at home on a VCR?

How did you feel about having to rewind the VHS tapes?

How much did it cost to rent a VHS movie from the video store?

Do you feel '80s movies had a realism, an optimism, or an innocent charm?

Do you consider the '80s to be the greatest decade for movies? Why or why not?

Television

List your top three '80s television sitcoms.

_____

_____

_____

Which '80s cartoons did you enjoy?

Did you rush home after school to watch TV? If so, which shows?

Did you refer to the "TV Guide" to learn when shows aired?

How many channels did your '80s television have?

Leisure Activities

'80s kids stayed physically active and were rarely sedentary. Kids skateboarded, biked everywhere, roller skated, explored the woods, and jumped in the pool.

What physical activities did you enjoy in the '80s?

Summer

Summer Vacations

Summer was a time for water balloon fights, BBQs, ice cream, popsicles, watching cartoons on Saturday mornings, and climbing trees.

What did you do during '80s summer vacations?

Family Vacations

Did your family vacation when school was out for the summer?

Describe one memorable family vacation spot.

If your family took road trips, what car games did you play?

Did your family consult large paper maps during road trips?

Did the family car have A/C?

What memories did family road trips create?

Bedroom

What posters hung on your '80s bedroom wall?

Did you have a uniquely shaped corded phone in your room? If so, describe it.

Did a lava lamp light up your bedroom with vibrant neon colors?

Did you have a TV—with a chunky remote—in your room?

Hobbies

What hobbies did you enjoy in the '80s?

Did you have any prize collections, like baseball cards, stamps, or coins?

Malls

Mall culture took center stage for '80s youth.

Was the mall a hotspot for you and your friends?

How often did you hang out at the mall?

What did you find alluring about walking around the sea of stores, kiosks, arcades, movie theaters, and eateries?

Jobs

Popular jobs for '80s kids included babysitter, fast food, and newspaper delivery.

If you worked in the '80s, what jobs did you hold?

How much did you earn?

What did you spend your earnings on?

Lemonade Stands

Did you operate a lemonade stand?

If so, how much did you charge per cup?

Did you turn a profit?

How did you advertise? Posterboard signs? Word-of-mouth?

143

Intangibles

What was your biggest takeaway of the decade?

What goals did you set for yourself in the '80s? Did you achieve them?

Describe one major accomplishment you are most proud of.

Did '80s culture give you any aha moments? If so, what was
one of them?

What about the '80s are you most grateful for?

In the '80s, who did you want to be, professionally or personally, when you grew up?

Who was your '80s hero, real or imagined? Why did you look up to them?

What emotions do you remember feeling most in the '80s?

What was an average day like in the '80s?

Describe your best, most unforgettable day.

Describe your worst, most forgettable day.

What aspects of the '80s excited you?

What values did you hold in the '80s?

Growing up in the '80s, what did you most want to change about the world?

What was the biggest risk you took in the '80s?

What would have made the '80s better than it was?

What about the '80s do you wish continued to the present day?

Sum up the '80s in one word.

_____

More Flashes from the '80s Past

More Flashes from the '80s Past

Long Live the '80s!

Answering these prompts might've returned you to simpler times, even if for a splendid moment. By sharing the completed journal, your loved ones gain insights into a slice of the irreplicable '80s culture that you are privileged to have been an important part of.

Now that's totally tubular!

Books in the
What Was It Like series

What Was It Like Growing Up in the 70s?
A Journal to Revisit and Share the Groovy 70s

What Was It Like During Christmas in the 80s?
A Journal to Revisit and Share the 80s Holiday Spirit

What Was It Like Fooding in the 80s?
A Journal to Revisit and Share 80s Totally Tubular Eats

What Was It Like Growing Up in the 90s?
A Journal to Revisit and Share the Rad 90s

What Was It Like During Christmas in the 90s?
A Journal to Revisit and Share the 90s Holiday Vibe

What Was It Like Marrying in the 90s?
A Journal (for Her) to Revisit and Share 90s Wedding
Magic